Made in the USA
Middletown, DE
07 October 2023

40416034R00057